WHAT'S
WRONG WITH
RELIGION?

Things No One Told You About Faith

SKYE JETHANI

What's Wrong with Religion: 9 Things No One Told You about Faith
© 2017 by Skye Jethani

All rights reserved. No part of this publication may be reproduced in any form without written permission from Skypilot Media, Wheaton, IL. www.skypilot.media

Unless otherwise noted, all scripture is taken from The Holy Bible, English Standard Version. ESV® Permanent Text Edition® (2016). Copyright © 2001 by Crossway Bibles, a publishing ministry of Good News Publishers.

The New Testament in Modern English by J. B. Phillips copyright © 1960, 1972 J. B. Phillips. Administered by The Archbishops Council of the Church of England. Used by permission.

Holy Bible, New International Version®, NIV® Copyright © 1973, 1978, 1984, 2011 by Biblica Inc.® Used by permission. All rights reserved worldwide.

ISBN 978-1-94429-823-4

Cover and interior design by Niddy Griddy Design, Inc.

LCCN 2017938933

Printed in the United States of America

1 2 3 4 5 6 7 8 9 10 Printing/Year 21 20 19 18 17

"Skye Jethani has written a clear, lucid, accessible guide to barriers that obstruct peoples' faith. Whatever your convictions about religion might be, if you are interested in ultimate questions these words will be a welcome help."

JOHN ORTBERG
BEST-SELLING AUTHOR AND SENIOR PASTOR OF MENLO PARK PRESBYTERIAN CHURCH

"Speaking to both the religious and irreligious, Skye cuts through the stereotypes to talk with hope, humor, and honesty about what's wrong with religion and what's right about faith. If you're disillusioned about religion you must read this book!"

BOB GOFF
AUTHOR OF LOVE DOES

"If you are serious about the religious quest and unsatisfied with the cookie-cutter institutions, give this book a fair hearing. But, don't let the clear images and the clever expressions get in the way of the seriousness of **What's Wrong with Religion?** The slower you read this book the better it gets."

SCOT MCKNIGHT
PROFESSOR OF NEW TESTAMENT

"Skye is a storyteller of ideas, with the rare ability to grip my imagination, sharpen my mind, and awaken my spirit. In **What's Wrong with Religion?** Skye tells the story of our conflicted relationship with faith, deftly deconstructing religion before giving us something better to believe in. Highly recommended to challenge the curious and the Christian alike."

PAUL J. PASTOR
AUTHOR OF THE LISTENING DAY: MEDITATIONS ON THE WAY

"Every page in **What's Wrong with Religion?** offers fresh insights for your life and faith. Skye uncovers the well-intentioned but toxic misunderstandings we have about Jesus and shines a powerful light on the WAY better life Jesus offers us all."

KARA POWELL
PHD, EXECUTIVE DIRECTOR OF THE FULLER YOUTH INSTITUTE AND
CO-AUTHOR OF GROWING YOUNG

"Refreshing, accessible, meaningful, and a helpful "religious" corrective for those swamped in a culture of cynicism, confusion and certitudes. I'd put this book into the hands of everyone at Mars Hill Bible Church."

A.J. SHERRILL
PASTOR OF MARS HILL BIBLE CHURCH

Skeptical about God? Exhausted by religion? If either statement describes you, Skye Jethani's latest book will feel like a cup of cool water. In **What's Wrong with Religion?** Jethani diagnoses the defective ways we approach God, whether it comes in the form of Pharisaic austerity or "cosmic bribery," and gently points to a better way. Ultimately, the book will help you exchange false burdens for Jesus' "easy yoke." I'll be recommending this book to both jaded skeptics and worn-out believers.

DREW DYCK IS AN EDITOR AT MOODY PUBLISHERS, CTPASTORS.COM
AND THE AUTHOR OF GENERATION EX-CHRISTIAN

"This book is absolutely fantastic. Skye takes you through a lightning fast overview of religion—why we love it, hate it, and just can't escape it no matter how "secular" we become as a society. Yet you never feel rushed or ripped off. It's engaging, smart, down to earth, funny, and above all, helpful for life. Long time follower of Jesus, or ardent hater of all things religious, and the many somewhere in between—read this book."

JOHN MARK COMER, PASTOR FOR TEACHING AND VISION AT BRIDGETOWN CHURCH
AND THE AUTHOR OF GOD HAS A NAME

for Billu

"Have mercy on those who doubt."
Jude 1:22

CONTENTS

"Most people play at religion as they play at games, religion itself being of all games the one most universally played."

A.W. TOZER

Intro: Religion Is a Game

It's not polite to talk about religion, so let's ease into the subject by talking about sports. Most people play sports for fun and many more watch it for entertainment. We want our children to at least try a sport and we sacrifice our weekends so they can, but we know most probably won't become professional athletes as adults. And that's ok. For most of us, sports has a place in our lives but it probably isn't a central one.

Religion functions the same way. We may have played with religion as kids, but now we just attend the big games or cheer for the home team in the playoffs. Some see religion as childish; a distraction from the serious business of life. They've outgrown it. But like sports, sometimes religion just cannot be ignored.

That's because some fans take it very, very seriously even if you do not. They identify intensely with their religious "team" and view all others as opponents. For them religion is more than a game—it is a battle. There was a time when entire communities or countries shared a single religion. It united people as they all cheered for the same team. Now, as people move and mix and morph, religion divides us more than it unites us, and sometimes it triggers conflicts and culture wars. That's why it's not polite to talk about it, and why some people stop playing the game all together.

Consider my family. In my diverse clan there are Hindus and humanists, evangelicals and atheists, Catholics and Cubs fans (yes, it's a religion too), Sikhs and skeptics. There were so many "teams" on the field, and so many conflicts between them, as a young man I was ready to abandon the game. It all seemed silly at best and dangerously toxic at worst.

Maybe you can relate.

That's when someone unexpected walked on to the field. He didn't come to play the game. In fact, he ignored it entirely. That is when I discovered the teaching and person of Jesus. I found him both incredibly offensive and outrageously attractive, and very different from the cultural and institutional "teams" that claimed his name.

This book outlines nine surprising things I've learned since I stopped playing the religion game and started following Jesus.

Let's begin...

EVERYONE IS RELIGIOUS

CHAPTER
1

The Mountain

I was 19 in Mumbai, India, when I found a tree with a shrine built around it. There were the usual assortment of animal-headed, multi-limbed Hindu gods represented, but I was surprised to see it included a verse from the Quran, the scriptures of Islam, an image of Moses holding the 10 Commandments, and another of Jesus.

The tree seemed to be saying, "It doesn't matter who or what you worship. Religions are all the same." It's a lovely sentiment and a popular one. We like to think about religions as paths up a mountain. Each culture has its own way of expressing spiritual truths, but ultimately the differences don't matter. Gandhi said it this way:

> "The various religions are like different roads converging on the same point. What difference does it make if we follow different routes, provided we all arrive at the same destination."
>
> MAHATMA GANDHI

Gandhi Was Wrong. (Yes, I said it.)

The idea that all spiritual paths lead to the same destination ignores each religion's unique teachings, culture, and history. It also misses the shared human struggle that motivates all religions. A more accurate picture turns the mountain upside down to show how **all religions start from the same place**.

Religions are how people in every culture respond to a world confused by chaos, plagued by scarcity, and corrupted by injustice. It's how we cope with our shared fear of death. To ease these fears, we all seek control over the world. Religions give us this sense of control.

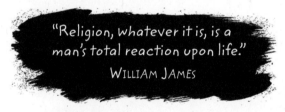

"Religion, whatever it is, is a man's total reaction upon life."
WILLIAM JAMES

From this starting place—our fears—different religious paths begin, but they splinter, multiply, and ultimately lead to very different places. Some paths are peaceful and others are violent. Some proclaim harmony and others discord. Some trust in gods and others put their trust in reason.

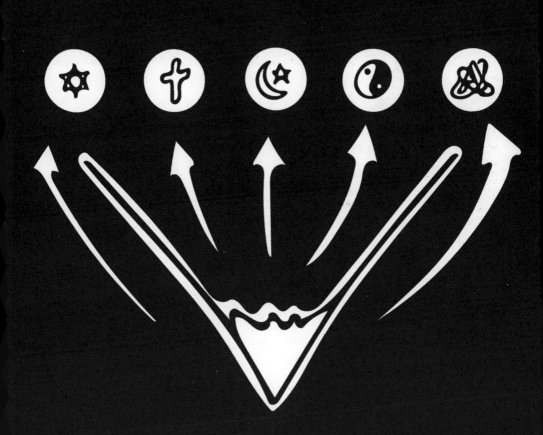

THE WILDERNESS

To better understand the shared origin of all religions, and why all people—
including the non-religious—are actually religious, let's look at the origin
story of just one. The beginning of the Hebrew Bible say that God created
the world as a place of order, beauty, and abundance. It was a garden paradise.

But that didn't last long. You probably know—or think you know—the
story of Adam and Eve. Pop culture says the story is about naughty naked
people with uncontrolled desires. It's not. The story is about people wanting
"to be like God." That is why they ate the forbidden fruit. God had intended
to rule over the earth *with* humanity, but the humans wanted to gain the
knowledge necessary to rule the world *instead of* God. It was a rebellion to
overthrow God and take his place.

It didn't end well. Humanity's relationship with God was broken and they
were thrown out of the garden into the wilderness.

In the ancient world, gardens were seen as places of order, beauty, and
abundance. They were safe. The wilderness, however, was feared as a realm
of chaos, ugliness, and scarcity. The story uses this imagery to make a simple
point: **Our world is a wilderness. That is why we are all afraid.**

Whatever you think about the Adam and Eve story, we can all agree that the world is a dangerous place. To ease our fears, we all strive to control the people and circumstances around us. The problem is that **the more we seek control over the world, the more dangerous it becomes.**

Here's a simple example. Imagine two tribes living in a desert with a single drinking well. Fear of dehydration leads each tribe to want control of the well, but access for one tribe means death for the other. Rather than eliminating their fears, seeking control of the well will only multiply them. Now the tribes have to fear both dehydration *and* war.

This is where religion enters the picture. **Religion gives us a sense of control over an uncontrollable world.** With rituals, prayers, morality, and missions, religions attempt to make sense out of the chaos we experience, and they provide us with ways to engage and manipulate the cosmos usually by controlling a god on our behalf.

Remember biology class? A frightened animal will respond in one of two ways: fight or flight. It will either run away from the danger or it will try to overpower the threat. Both fight and flight are attempts at control rooted in fear.

So is religion.

Depending on which religious path you take, it will either lead you to seek control over the dangers of the world by

> "War is the normal occupation of man. War...and gardening."
> WINSTON CHURCHILL

running away, or it will guide you to gain control by fighting to make the world into what you (or your god) want it to be.

The problem, as we saw with the tribes fighting to control the well, is that **seeking control only makes the world a more dangerous place.** We get caught in a loop of danger, fear, and control that never ends. So, when we discover that one religious path is a dead end, we try another, and another. Eventually, we may give up on religion entirely, but that doesn't mean we've escaped the wilderness.

The Ultimate

The popular perception is that religion is unnecessary in the modern world, and that's why its influence is declining. Never mind that evidence shows the world is actually becoming *more* religious. In your community being religious is probably viewed as odd or even extreme. You'll hear people say, "I'm spiritual but not religious." It's their way of saying, "I'm deep but not crazy."

What no one told you, and what most people refuse to believe, is that **everyone is religious**. Why? Because everyone experiences the same dangerous world, everyone becomes afraid, and everyone looks for a way to overcome their fears through a system of control. Their way up the mountain may not be the path of a traditional religion, but that doesn't mean they're not trying to solve the same problem religions were created to solve.

Paul Tillich, a philosopher and theologian, said that to

> "Faith is the state of being ultimately concerned."
> PAUL TILLICH

be human is to be religious because **everyone has something of *ultimate concern***. Some call their ultimate concern "God," for others it may be fame, wealth, power, sex, a relationship, a country, or a cause. Each person's ultimate concern functions as their god. It gives them a sense of meaning, purpose, and—you guessed it—*control* in a fearful world.

In Tillich's view, both the religious and non-religious are traveling up the inverted mountain. The only question is, which path will break the cycle of danger, fear, and control we are all trying to escape?

Q: *What is your ultimate concern and how does it provide you with a sense of meaning and control?*

How Religion Ruins the World

CHAPTER

2

The Puppet

Religions do some strange things. They dunk fully clothed people under water. They make millions of people walk around a huge black cube seven times. They throw virgins down volcanos. I once awoke in a foreign country to discover a religious ceremony happening in my bedroom involving a man balancing a dish on his head containing water, flowers, and a flaming coconut while surrounded by four dancing eunuchs.

Why the strange rituals? Early civilizations believed the cosmos was managed by deities—gods with personalities, wills, and tempers. So, if you wanted to gain control over the world to protect yourself or your community from harm, you had to gain control over the gods controlling the world.

Early religions used sacrifices and rituals to appease the anger of some gods and win the blessing of others. **Religion was basically cosmic bribery.** Sacrifices were how people controlled divine forces and participated in keeping the universe functioning.

We know the sun rises each morning because the earth has completed another rotation on its axis, but ancient people thought the sun rose because a god *willed* it to rise. Some even believed the sun itself was a god. Therefore,

25

if the sun god became angry he may not return tomorrow. To diminish this fear, and many others, religion provided a way to control the temper tantrums of the gods. Cue the eunuchs.

As religion evolved so did its systems of control. Rather than rituals, incantations, and sacrifices, in time morality also became an important way of winning divine favor or escaping divine wrath.

Living within moral parameters ensured that your crops were plentiful, your family prospered, and your community avoided war and famine. For this reason many religious people appear devoted to God by humbly submitting to his commands. But a closer look can reveal a very different picture.

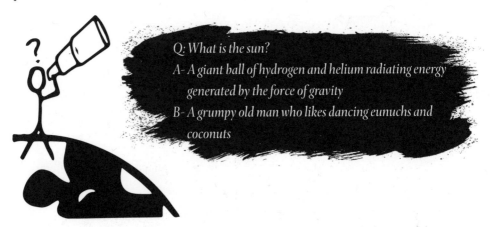

Q: What is the sun?
A- A giant ball of hydrogen and helium radiating energy generated by the force of gravity
B- A grumpy old man who likes dancing eunuchs and coconuts

Rather than loving devotion, a religious person may simply be afraid of the dangers that fill our unpredictable world. *Will I get the job? Will my kids be ok? Will my team win the semifinals?* To gain control over these uncontrollable things, **the religious person tries to win God's favor through moral behavior.** The person may *appear* devoted to God, but in reality she is trying to control him like a puppet in order to manipulate the world in her favor.

Consider this tweet from NFL wide receiver Stevie Johnson after he dropped a pass in the end zone. Johnson did his part—he praised God. In exchange he expected God to help him catch footballs. When the Almighty appeared to not keep his end of the bargain, Johnson blasted God on social media.

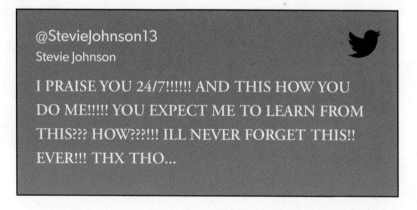

@StevieJohnson13
Stevie Johnson

I PRAISE YOU 24/7!!!!!! AND THIS HOW YOU DO ME!!!!! YOU EXPECT ME TO LEARN FROM THIS??? HOW???!!! ILL NEVER FORGET THIS!! EVER!!! THX THO...

Johnson's tweet illustrates the first problem with religion—**God doesn't play ball with our attempts to control him.** But if God can't be controlled, why do so many people still try?

It's called **confirmation bias**. Religions like to tell the stories of how prayers/rituals/morality have won God's favor in the past, but they usually ignore the stories of God's silence or non-cooperation. Consider Diagoras, an atheist philosopher in ancient Greece. To convince him the gods were real, he was shown pictures of sailors who prayed and were later saved from a shipwreck. Diagoras was not impressed. He asked, "Where are the pictures of those who prayed but drowned?" Dead people usually don't share their stories of the gods' unfaithfulness.

By highlighting only the positive stories, religions construct the perception that they have the power to control the universe, and fearful people looking for solutions line up to buy what religious leaders are selling.

I saw this vividly as a teenager. Adolescents are among the most fearful and insecure people. So, when a religious leader tells young people that in exchange for their sexual abstinence God will bless their grades, their relationships, and even their future careers and marriages, it provides a sense of control during an out-of-control season of life. These messages are usually followed by the glowing testimonies of couples that have been married for

DIAGORAS' DOUBT

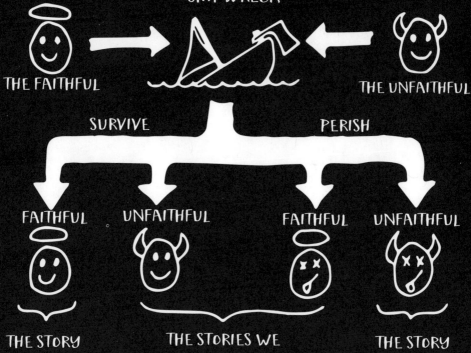

SHIPWRECK

THE FAITHFUL

THE UNFAITHFUL

SURVIVE

PERISH

FAITHFUL

UNFAITHFUL

FAITHFUL

UNFAITHFUL

THE STORY
WE ARE TOLD

THE STORIES WE
ARE NOT TOLD

THE STORY
WE ASSUME

about two minutes. What's never shared are the stories of teenage celibates whose future marriages struggle or end in divorce.

These moral formulas create a no-win situation. Either a person will conform to every moral boundary and eventually discover that God won't be manipulated to fulfill all of their dreams, or (more likely) a person will fail to stay within the moral boundaries and conclude they are beyond God's blessing.

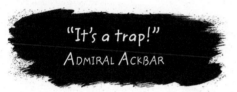

"It's a trap!"
ADMIRAL ACKBAR

Is it any wonder why so many young adults are abandoning religion?

THE POLICE

If we believe avoiding calamity is achieved by rigorously obeying religious rules, then religious leaders must function as a divine police force to keep everyone in line. They become God's Gestapo. We imagine the ruler-slapping nun or the anal-retentive reverend wagging his finger at teenagers saying, "Don't smoke, or chew, or date girls that do!" In truth, where a fear-based view of religion is held, strict clergy are usually deeply respected.

By keeping each person within the boundaries, the priestly police are securing the welfare of the entire community. Why risk God's wrath upon the whole town just because Kevin Bacon wants to dance?

Sadly, this instinct to impose what is believed to be God's will upon a community for its own good has led to many horrors. Consider the terrorist attacks on September 11, 2001. Three years earlier, Al-Qaeda issued a declaration saying America was defying God's will by putting soldiers in the Arabian Peninsula. The terrorists believed they were acting as God's police by punishing America for violating his laws.

Amazingly, there were some religious Americans who agreed with them. Days after the attacks, a well-known church leader declared on national television: "I really believe that the pagans, and the abortionists, and the feminists, and the gays and the lesbians...all of them who have tried to secularize America. I point the finger in their face and say 'you helped this happen.'"

Muslim terrorists and Christian fundamentalists both believed 9/11 happened because America had violated God's commands—they just disagreed over *which* commands.

Atheists like Christopher Hitchens pounce on the horrors committed by religions to argue against the existence of God. Hitchens debated former British prime minister and Roman Catholic, Tony Blair, about the value of religion. In the debate, Blair highlighted the many compassionate actions of religious believers throughout history, but Hitchens countered by listing religious atrocities committed by those acting as God's police.

After the debate, the audience was polled to determine the winner. The atheist won handily.

> 68% said religion is a more destructive than benign force in the world.
> HITCHENS-BLAIR DEBATE 2010

THE BURDEN

Christopher Hitchens was the kind of person Jesus would have spent time with. Like Hitchens, Jesus also had serious problems with religious leaders who acted like God's police. The scribes and Pharisees of Jesus' time carried a very simple, but very burdensome, understanding of religion:

$$Obedience = Blessing$$
$$Disobedience = Cursing$$

These equations meant those who appeared blessed (the rich, healthy, and powerful) were viewed as being rewarded by God for their obedience. The cursed (the poor, sick, and powerless) were viewed as getting what they deserved for their disobedience. The world had winners and losers. The scribes and Pharisees were winners. Jesus and his ragtag band of hillbilly fishermen and prostitutes were the losers.

Jesus challenged this simple formula. For example, the religious leaders assumed that a man was born blind because someone in his family had disobeyed God. To prove that was not the case, Jesus restored the man's sight and said the man was actually blessed (John 9). On the flip side, Jesus said wealth could be a curse and a barrier to God rather than a blessing. To the shock of the religious leaders, and even his own followers, Jesus said it was easier for a camel to go through the eye of a needle than for a rich person to live with God. (Matthew 19:24).

But he saved his nastiest criticism for the religious leaders themselves.

RELIGION'S BURDEN   JESUS' BURDEN

(For those who think Jesus was only meek and mild, read Matthew 23.) Jesus' real problem with the religious leaders was that, "They tie up heavy burdens, hard to bear, and lay them on people's shoulder." These burdens were the rituals, sacrifices, and moral codes used to control God. In ancient Israel, religious requirements were called a "yoke"—the apparatus put on an animal's shoulders to pull a wagon or plough.

To those tired of religion's heavy yoke, Jesus said, "Come to me, all who labor and are heavy laden, and I will give you rest. Take my yoke upon you, and learn from me, for I am gentle and lowly in heart, and you will find rest for your souls. For my yoke is easy, and my burden is light" (Matthew 11:28-30).

Religion ruins the world by making us believe we can control God. This, in turn, makes us want to control one another. It turns fearful people into tyrants and religious communities into police states. The solution seems obvious—let's get rid of religion. In the next chapter we'll see why that's a bad idea.

Q: How have you tried to control God? How did you discover that religious systems of control don't work?

GETTING RID
of RELIGION
DOESN'T HELP

The Line

Like medieval doctors drilling holes into skulls to cure a fever, mere religion does nothing to solve what infects humanity and sometimes manages to makes things worse. Religion's bad track record has led many to conclude that getting rid of it is the only answer.

A few years ago, I was visiting the beach in California with my family. Our peaceful day was interrupted by a group of street preachers standing on crates holding signs and shouting into bullhorns, but I was surprised to discover they were zealously preaching repentance from *religion*. They were atheists who believed religion was ruining the world. Are they right? Is religion what's wrong with the world, and will abandoning it save humanity?

I don't think so.

Think about those medieval, skull-drilling doctors. Ending that barbaric practice was a good idea because putting holes in heads doesn't cure fevers, but not drilling holes didn't cure any fevers either. **There is a difference between giving up a failed solution and actually solving the problem.** Likewise, religion may not solve humanity's problems, but removing religion's bad medicine won't solve our problems either. The last century has shown that atheism is not the miracle cure its devotees believe it to be.

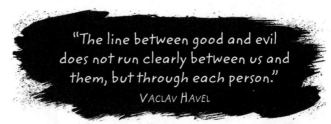

90 Million: estimated number of people killed by atheist regimes in the 20th century.

Many of the most oppressive regimes of the 20th century were constructed on a foundation of atheism. Stalin's Soviet Union, Mao's Cultural Revolution in China, the Khmer Rouge in Cambodia, and the ongoing horrors in North Korea were all murderous atheistic regimes.

Religious people are capable of terrible evil, but removing religion does not make us better. It simply replaces a religious motive for evil with a non-religious motive for evil.

Vaclav Havel understood this. After being imprisoned by the Communists, he was later elected president of the Czech Republic. Rather than destroying his political enemies, Havel surprised many by forgiving them. He said,

"The line between good and evil does not run clearly between us and them, but through each person."
VACLAV HAVEL

THEM

EVIL

US

GOOD

Some may kill in the name of God, but the last century has shown that just as many people are willing to kill in the name of a political leader, country, philosophy, or economic system. **Religion is not the problem. We are.**

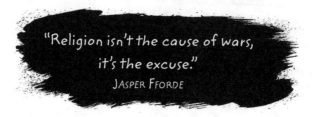

"Religion isn't the cause of wars, it's the excuse."
JASPER FFORDE

THE ARCHITECT

A recent poll of 65 countries found that only 11 percent of people are "convinced atheists." That's down from 13 percent just three years earlier. Almost nine out of ten people globally believe in God and the number is growing. A big win for religion, right?

Not exactly.

Acknowledging the existence of God isn't the same as being devoted to him. A case can be made that even those who identify as "religious" don't actually have their values or vision of the world shaped in any meaningful way by faith. They may still be "functional atheists." **You don't have to *be* an atheist to live like one.**

Functional atheism has another name: *deism*. Deism says God exists and created the cosmos, but he's no longer involved in human affairs. Imagine the world as a bustling skyscraper full of offices, apartments, and restaurants. Deists view God as the architect. He designed the whole building and may have overseen its construction, but his job is now done. He's handed over the day-to-day management of the building to us.

A lot of us have inherited this view of God from our culture. For example, when you get a fever the thought of visiting a priest for prayer is about as likely to enter your brain as a medieval hand drill. Instead, you will go to the pharmacy for a drug. Rather than trying to control the world through religion's superstitious methods (rituals, sacrifices, and morality), our more enlightened age has taught us to take direct control of the world through tested principles, formulas, and a knowledge of natural laws. Science has cut God and religion out of everyday life. Seeing God as a distant architect explains why so many can worship him on Sunday but live as if he doesn't exist on Monday.

11% of people worldwide are "convinced atheists" (the other 89% may be "functional atheists").

The Blueprints

What is the Bible? I asked that question in a church once and an eager teenager said that, "B.I.B.L.E. stand for Basic Instruction Before Leaving Earth." I've also heard well-meaning people describe it as "God's manual for the human being." These remarks are intended to show the Bible's value. Ironically, these comments are also profoundly unbiblical.

When God is viewed as the world's architect, it makes sense to see the Bible as his blueprints. Just as he established the laws of gravity, the laws of thermodynamics, and the laws of mathematics, religious people assume he also created immutable laws to govern other areas of life like leadership, relationships, and business. Some of God's laws are revealed through the scientific exploration of nature, but others are revealed in the pages of scripture.

When the Bible is seen this way, as a book of divine principles for life, it completely changes the way we engage it. Rather than a vehicle for knowing God and fostering our communion with *him*, we search the the Bible for practical *principles* we may use to control our world, and God himself becomes entirely optional. In other words, **some religious people have**

WHAT IS THE BIBLE?

WINDOW

OR

MANUAL

THROUGH IT I DISCOVER
HOW TO SEE GOD, MYSELF
AND HIS WORLD

THROUGH IT I DISCOVER
HOW TO MANAGE MY
LIFE AND MY WORLD

PRODUCES

A DESIRE
FOR GOD

A DESIRE
FOR CONTROL

=

=

RELATIONSHIP

RELIGION

confused a relationship with the Bible for a relationship with the God *of* the Bible. They are not the same thing.

Don't get me wrong, I think the Bible is immensely important, and it does contain many important truths we should apply to our world. But in their zeal for the scriptures, some religious communities actually reduce the Bible from the story that reveals God to us, to merely a collection of divine principles for life.

This was an error made by religious people in Jesus' time. They memorized every commandment in the Bible and tried to apply every principle. But their knowledge of God's words did not help them recognize God himself when he was standing right in front of them. In fact, they rejected, tortured, and killed him.

Like atheists and deists, many religious people also push God aside in order to take more direct control over their lives. They reduce faith to a set of principles and simple applications: 4 *Steps to a Lasting Marriage, How to Raise Kids the*

"You search the Scriptures because you think in them you have eternal life; and it is they that bear witness about me, yet you refuse to come to me that you may have life."
JESUS (JOHN 5:39-40)

THE CHRISTIAN DEIST CHECKLIST

- [ ] BIBLICAL EDUCATION
- [ ] BIBLICAL ETHICS
- [ ] BIBLICAL POLITICS
- [ ] BIBLICAL FAMILY
- [ ] BIBLE TEACHING CHURCH
- [ ] BIBLE STUDY GROUP
- [ ] JESUS CHRIST (OPTIONAL)

Bible's Way, Jesus' Plan for Successful Leadership, Kingdom Financial Management, etc. But knowing and practicing these principles does not actually require God to be involved.

Today, being a Christian can mean you've exchanged some secular set of principles for life with a new set of ideas taken from the Bible. God may be celebrated and thanked for giving us his instructions for life, but like the absent architect, God's presence in one's life remains entirely optional.

Despite advances in science and our less superstitious brand of religion, the same scarcity, ugliness, and injustice that plagued earlier generations still plagues ours. And in some places where religion is abandoned altogether the world can actually get worse. History has shown that the choice between religion or no religion is like the choice between being shot or being poisoned. Neither system of control can break the cycles of fear and danger the infect our world.

> *Q: How do you seek direct control over your life? If you are religious, how has God become optional to your preferred system of control?*

GOD DOES NOT EXIST TO BE USED . . .

CHAPTER

4

THE MAKEOVER

On January 20, 1804, Thomas Jefferson ordered two Bibles from a Philadelphia bookstore. When they arrived, the President turned to the gospels and used a razor to literally cut out all of the passages about Jesus he did not like. When he finished only ten percent of the original text remained. All of Jesus' miracles, his divine birth, his sacrificial death, and his resurrection were left on the White House floor.

With these pesky bits out of the way, Jefferson was able to reassemble a Jesus that fit his own ideas about democracy and philosophy. He was able to create a Jesus that looked more like himself. Despite rejecting nearly all of Jesus' words and actions Jefferson insisted, "I am a true Christian...a disciple of the doctrines of Jesus." That's like claiming to be a true vegetarian because you only eat grass-fed beef.

Like Jefferson, **most of us remake God in our own image all the time.** Scot McKnight, a professor in Chicago, gave his students a 24-question survey at the start of every semester to assess their view of Jesus. Later in the semester, McKnight compared their answers with another 24-question survey students completed about their own views and personalities. When he compared the answers the outcome was remarkably consistent. Everyone thought Jesus was just like themselves.

Except you.

Surely you're not that narcissistic. You wouldn't cut and paste God to fit your political beliefs like Jefferson. You don't assume that God agrees with all of your social or moral views like McKnight's students. Take a moment to think of just one opinion you hold that you're certain God disagrees with.

Need more time?

Ok, maybe you are that narcissistic. We all are. As we've already learned, religion is appealing because it offers us a sense of control in a dangerous world, but **a sense of control only lasts as long as God looks, acts, thinks, and judges like me.** Therefore, when God doesn't look like me a divine makeover is necessary.

We do this because we're afraid of losing control. If God is just like me then I am safe; I am still in control. I know what to expect from the world and the God who controls it, and I don't have to change. If God is different from me,

> "If God has made us in his image, we have returned him the favor."
> VOLTAIRE

however, then I'm in trouble. Such a God might expect me to change, and that's not the kind of religion most people want.

The King

So, what kind of religion do people want? That question was answered by a team from the University of North Carolina researching the beliefs of teenagers. They concluded that most American teens view God as a "combination divine butler and cosmic therapist," and teens were "primarily concerned with one's own happiness in contrast to focusing on glorifying God, learning obedience, or serving others." This was the religion of most teens, the researchers concluded, because it is also the form of religion practiced by their parents.

Americans want a god who will serve our needs, fix our problems, and help us achieve our goals. We want to *use* God in the same way we use a personal trainer or a vending machine. In other words, **we have come to view religion the way we view everything else—as *consumers*.**

CONSUMER WORSHIP

In a consumer culture nothing has intrinsic value. Instead, the value of a product, or a person, or a religion is in it's usefulness. Is your car/spouse/god failing to meet your desires? Trade it in for a new model, or at the very least give it a makeover. Such transactional ethics are acceptable because **in our culture the self and its desires are the uncontested center of the universe.**

This explains why so many religious institutions market God as a miracle product that will transform your life. In such places worship isn't primarily an act of thanksgiving or devotion, but an act of consumption. People gather to be entertained by the music and helped by the sermon, and if attendance declines the leaders of the organization will quickly survey their customers to find out how to improve their offering.

In this consumeristic approach to religion our desires are never questioned or challenged. A desire is never judged as right or wrong; it is only seen as met or unmet. Likewise, in consumer religion you do not exist to serve God. Instead, he exists to serve you because the customer is always king.

> "Advertising signs: they con you into thinking you're the one
> That can do what's never been done That can win what's
> never been won Meantime life outside goes on all around you"
> BOB DYLAN

THE CONSUMER COSMOS

GOD

SELF

OTHERS

The Brat

Consumerism is a modern idea, but the view that God exists to be used is as old as religion itself. While at a dinner party, Jesus told a story about a selfish son to illustrate the problem with this approach to God. (The story is recorded in Luke 15). The son, Jesus said, asked his father for his inheritance *in advance*. Yeah, he was basically telling his dad to "drop dead." Once the son had the cash, he left his father's home and "squandered his property in reckless living" in a distant country.

In the story, the father represents God and the son represents how many of us relate to him. Like the self-centered young man, most of us aren't genuinely interested in God. Instead, we're focused on what we can get *from* him. **We expect God to help us fulfill our dreams and desires. He is merely a tool; a device we use to achieve some greater goal.**

To be fair, unlike the brat in the story whose goals appeared limited to women and wine, some of us have more admirable ambitions. Surely God doesn't mind if we use him to achieve good things, right?

It's not that simple. **Our desires aren't always the problem, but how we order them.** When we desire something more than God, even a good thing, two things happen. First, whatever we desire most—whatever is our "ultimate concern" (remember that from Ch. 1?)—that thing will become our god. When something other than the Creator occupies this place in our life it is called an *idol*. Idolatry is simply worshipping what is created rather than the Creator.

Second, we will expect God to serve our idol as well, just as the son wanted to use his father to fund his wild living. **The Creator of the universe, however, is not a slave who willingly submits to our idolatrous dreams.** For example, Jesus said, "Whoever loves father or mother more than me is not worthy of me, and whoever loves son or daughter more than me is not worthy of me" (Matthew 10:37). He was attacking our tendency to make a good thing, like family, into an ultimate thing. He went on to warn about the idols of wealth (Matthew 6:19-24), comfort (Luke 9:58), and fame (Matthew 6:1-4). None of

these are bad things; in fact each can be very good, but none are to be more important than God.

> "Idolatry is turning a good thing into an ultimate thing."
> TIMOTHY KELLER

Presenting God as a useful product is an easy way to make religion appealing in a consumer culture, and remaking God in our own image will give us the temporary illusion of control we crave. Both of these approaches, however, are really ways of worshipping ourselves rather than God.

Q: How have you tried to use God to achieve your "dreams"? How have you seen this approach used by religious institutions to win followers?

SON → DESIRES

...AND NEITHER Do You

CHAPTER

5

THE ACTIVIST COSMOS

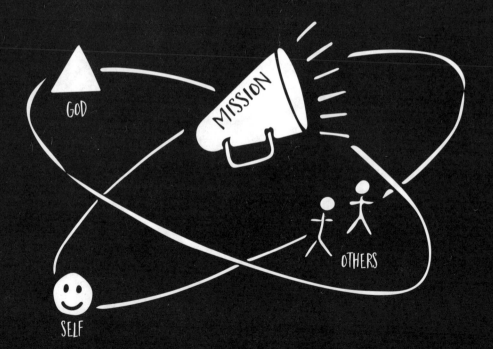

GOD

MISSION

OTHERS

SELF

The Pagans

Why are we here? In nearly every ancient creation myth humans were formed to serve the gods. People supplied the gods with food through their sacrifices, built temples to be the gods' homes, and fought battles for their king who was seen as a god on earth. Humans were the gods' servants.

This pagan vision of humanity was turned upside down by the creation story of ancient Israel. Their God was different. He did not need to be fed, housed, and pampered like the gods of Babylon or Greece. "If I were hungry, I would not tell you," he said, "for the world and its fullness are mine" (Psalm 50:12). And he made clear that he does not live in a temple built by people. Instead the whole cosmos was his home (Isaiah 66:1). In other words, Israel's God did not *need* people. Therefore, in their creation story **humans are not God's servants but his representatives.** "God created man in his own image...male and female he created them" (Genesis 1:27).

"I need you to need me."
CHEAP TRICK LYRIC
(& MOTTO OF PAGANS EVERYWHERE)

This not only elevated the dignity of all people, it also undermined the purpose of religion.

Earlier we defined religion as a system of control rooted in fear. But how do you control a God that doesn't need anything? And **what's the point of religion if you can't control God?**

Maybe that's why so many people still prefer the pagan approach. We'd rather see ourselves as servants upon whom God depends.

In the last chapter, we looked at our consumer instinct to use God as a self-improvement product. The opposite view is also popular. **Rather than using God to achieve your goals, some insist we should be used *by* God to achieve *his* goals**. At first this appears logical and even devout. After all, it's arrogant to put yourself at the center of the universe. True religion, some say, is about sacrifice and dedication to a higher calling. The spotlight rightfully belongs on God's mission rather than your dreams.

Religions may disagree about what exactly the mission is, but most put some great work that was started by God and is now being carried forward by his servants at the center of the universe. Every person is then viewed in relationship to this mission. Those who devote their lives to the mission are celebrated, while those who are distracted by less divine work are judged or quietly shamed.

Ironically, in their attempt to remove our culture's idol of consumerism, many religious people have exchanged it for another idol called *missionalism*, and they've become even more pagan in the process

Missionalism
[mi-shuh-nl-iz-uh m] noun
1. the belief that the worth of one's life is determined by the achievement of a great goal started by God.
2. a form of idol worship practiced by religious people who complain about the culture's focus on consumerism.

The Bomb

Daisy cutter is the nickname for the military's largest non-nuclear bomb. It was first used during the Vietnam War to clear jungles for helicopter landing zones. Despite having laser-guided smart bombs, the military still uses the old daisy cutters. The reason is simple. Nothing terrifies the enemy like the shock and awe of a 15,000 pound bomb. Daisy cutters are all about impact.

MISSIONALISM

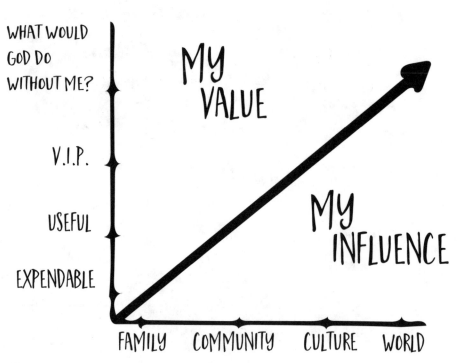

Impact is also highly valued by religious communities that have made God's mission into an idol. I call it the Daisy Cutter Doctrine. I see this belief carried by many young adults, including those who do not consider themselves religious. Much has been written about the allure of social activism among the young today. No doubt many are driven by a pure desire to alleviate the injustices they see in our world, but is that the only motivation at work?

Our culture bombards young people with messages about "changing the world." In fact, the number of books with that phrase in the title has grown exponentially in recent years, as have the number of young adults who struggle with depression when they haven't become celebrities who've impacted the world by age 30.

Consider the research of Dr. Brad Bushman. His team found that college students receive more pleasure from having their self-esteem boosted than

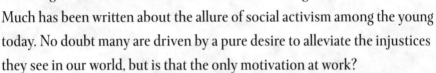

from sex, alcohol, or money. "It is somewhat surprising how this desire to feel worthy and valuable trumps almost any other pleasant activity you can imagine," Bushman concluded. We desperately want to matter. **Religion says our aching sense of insignificance can be overcome if we just do more for God.** Sometimes the message comes as a warning to "not waste your life" in a secular occupation, or to "live in light of eternity" by focusing on God's mission.

A few years ago, I heard a church leader speaking to an arena of college students say, "The only thing I am afraid of is living an insignificant life." And he defined a significant life was as one that measurably impacts the world for God.

BOOM!

Another daisy cutter detonated and 20,000 young people were flattened by the burden to change the world.

The (Other) Brat

So, what's wrong with wanting to change the world for God? Nothing, of course, unless you think God's mission needs more reality TV shows or special Christmas albums. (We have enough of those.) The world needs changing. **The problem is when we fall into the pagan view that God needs us or that our value is defined by our usefulness.**

In the last chapter we looked at Jesus' story about the selfish son who squandered his father's wealth on wild living. The son represents **religious consumerism**—the view that God exists to be used to achieve our desires. But that's only half of the story. Jesus said the father had another son. He was very different from his younger brother—at least on the surface. The older son was obedient and reliable. By all appearances he was the "good son."

Appearances can be deceiving.

When the rebellious younger son returned home, the father threw a party and the older son threw a tantrum. "All these years I have served you," he whined, "I've done everything you've asked and you never gave me a party. But your other son, who wasted your money on gambling and prostitutes, gets a feast! Seriously?" It's difficult not to sympathize with the older son, but

69

he's not the hero of Jesus' story. In fact, Jesus presents the "good son" as *more* lost than the "bad son."

The older son represents **religious activism**—the view that we exist to be used by God. Notice where the older son puts his significance. He lived *for* his father and he expected a reward for his service.

Once we see their ultimate motivations, we discover how similar the two sons really are. Neither was interested in a relationship with their father. Instead, they were both focused on what they might receive from him. While the young son simply took what he desired, the older son worked for it. Similarly, while religious consumerism and activism appear very different, beneath the surface they are identical. They are both idols that make something other than God ultimately important.

OLDER SON   FATHER   YOUNGER SON

ACTIVISM   CONSUMERISM

It's interesting that Jesus told the story of the two sons at a dinner party with religious leaders—men who devoted their lives to obeying

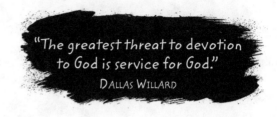

"The greatest threat to devotion to God is service for God."

DALLAS WILLARD

God's commands and advancing his mission. It was a room full of older sons. Was Jesus diminishing the importance of the older son's service or endorsing the younger son's sinfulness? Of course not. **The story serves as a warning to those who think the goal is transforming religious consumers into religious activists**, but that is exactly the goal within many faith communities.

Jesus wanted his listeners to grasp what so many of us miss: **What God cares most about is not your obedience nor your disobedience but your** *presence*.

Q: How have you linked your value to your impact in the world?
   How are these messages communicated by your community?

THE SOLUTION:
LIVING WITH GOD

GOD EXISTS IN ETERNAL RELATIONSHIP

WITH HIMSELF

THE PARTY

Only at the very end of the story of the lost sons are we offered an explanation for the father's behavior. Why did he run and embrace his younger son? Why did he throw a party for him? Why did he not reward his older son's years of service? All of these questions are answered when the father finally responds to the older son's anger. "Son," he says, "you are always with me, and all that is mine is yours. It was fitting to celebrate and be glad, for this brother of yours was dead, and is alive; he was lost, and is found" (Luke 15:31-32).

Did you catch it? The meaning of the entire story hinges on a single word—*with*.

While the sons were both obsessed with money, pleasures, honors, or rewards, the father was obsessed with *his sons*. This explains why he ran to hug the younger son and why he threw the party. It had nothing to do with the younger son's behavior, and everything to do with the father's joy at having his boy with him again. Similarly, what mattered most to the father wasn't the older son's years of service, but his years of faithful presence. "You are always *with* me."

This is the turning point in Jesus' story, and it's the turning point of this book.

For five chapters we've been asking: *What's wrong with religion?* We have seen how religion, while promising to remove our fears, only makes the world a more dangerous place. We've seen that escaping religion isn't possible because everyone is religious and anything can be our god. We've seen how using God to achieve our dreams is just consumerism wearing a spiritual disguise. And we've seen how a drive to "change the world" for God is actually a step backward into pagan utilitarianism.

None of these common approaches to religion escapes the cycle of danger, fear, and control that defines our world and our lives, because none of them sees God correctly.

This is what makes Jesus' message so surprising. Jesus declared that if we peel back the layers of religious tradition, if we could gaze back before creation to a time before time itself when there was nothing but God, we would not discover a mission, or our dreams, not even moral or natural laws. We would see **love**.

But how is that possible? For love to exist there must be both a lover and a beloved; there must be a relationship. It takes two to tango, as they say. This has led some to incorrectly believe that God created people because he was lonely and needed someone to love, but as we saw in the last chapter God doesn't *need* anyone. Instead, Jesus affirmed something far more amazing; a vision of God that would forever change how people relate to him. He said that **God himself is a community of perfect love**.

The New Testament speaks of God as a **Trinity** (the word comes from *tri-*, meaning three, and *-unity*, meaning one). God is one *and* he eternally exists in three persons—God the Father, God the Son, and God the Holy Spirit. It's a paradox beyond human logic and a mystery beyond the scope of this small book. However, a basic understanding of the Trinity is essential if we are to grasp what makes Jesus' message about God's love so remarkable.

Robert Farrar Capon described the Trinity as an eternal party—one God in three persons experiencing joy, love, and unity together on a level we cannot begin to fathom. Creation was the overflow of this divine bash; the result of God's love bursting beyond the boundaries of the Trinity to

> "God did not create in order to be loved, but rather, created out of the overflow of the perfect love that had always existed among Father, Son, and Holy Spirit who ever live in perfect and mutual relationship and delight."
> KEVIN DEYOUNG

create stars and planets and people. **A trinitarian vision of God means the foundation of our universe is not material but *relational*.**

Jesus' prayer for his followers was rooted in this idea. He prayed: "Just as you, Father, are in me, and I in you, that they also may be in us" (John 17:21). Like the father in his story who invited the older son to come join the celebration, Jesus wants us to join the party the Trinity has been throwing since before creation began. He wants us to share in the loving relationship between God the Father, Son, and Spirit. More than anything, God wants us to be *with* him.

The Goal

I used to have this pin on my computer bag. (It disappeared in a bag scanner at the Denver airport.)

Being in the business of words, the pin reminded me that simply declaring something does not make it true EVEN IF IT'S WRITTEN IN ALL CAPS WITH AN EXCLAMATION MARK! If you spend much time

THIS IS NOT A PIN!

among religious people of a certain tradition, sooner or later you'll hear talk about having "a personal relationship with God." That sounds great, but **saying you have a relationship with God is not the same as *having* one.**

For example, I've spoken with students at many colleges where having a relationship with Jesus is often a requirement for admission, but when I dig beyond the clichés to determine what their connection with God actually looks like, many students have little to say. Some will mention things they know *about* God—a bit of theology or a lyric they picked up from a song— while others will talk of God the way an office worker speaks about the CEO he's never met but whose portrait is on the wall. They show respect and maybe even a commitment to service, but a personal connection with God isn't evident.

Increasingly, I'm meeting students who are ready to give up on the whole charade. They know how to *appear* religious, most learned how as children, but as young adults they're ready to admit they've never really felt connected to God.

I don't fault the students. Despite being immersed in religious households and institutions that talk about a "relationship with God," most were never presented a ravishing vision of God to awaken a genuine desire to know him. Remember my pin? Saying something, even repeatedly, doesn't make it true. **The message most young people hear instead is a call to *use* God rather than to love him.** It goes something like this:

> ### The Call to Use (Rather than to Love) God:
>
> A – You are destined for an eternity in hell because of your sins.
>
> B – God has paid the price for you by sending his Son, Jesus, to die on the cross in your place.
>
> C – If you believe in him your sins will be forgiven and you will spend eternity in heaven.

Does this sound familiar? It comes in different forms depending on one's religious culture. Old fashioned, fire and brimstone preachers will emphasize point A. More therapeutic ministers will downplay point A, or ignore it all together, to focus on points B and C. Regardless of how this message is presented, it is important to see that its ultimate goal is *not* a relationship with God. Instead, God is merely *how* one reaches the real goal which is entering heaven and/or avoiding hell. This is why we see endless religious movies about the coming apocalypse, and why travel guides by those claiming to have returned from heaven become best-sellers. **People fixated on heaven and hell, however, are missing the message of Jesus.**

HEAVEN

GOD △

Yes, Jesus came to "take away the sins of the world" (John 1:29, Phillips) and to "give his life as a ransom for many" (Mark 10:45), but the goal of his sacrifice on our behalf was not to get us into heaven. His goal was to reconcile us *to God*. Occupying heaven is merely the byproduct of being united with our Heavenly Father who dwells there. If we make heaven itself the goal, we miss the whole point. John Piper put it bluntly: "People who would be happy in heaven if Christ were not there, will not be there." Without God, after all, heaven is not heaven.

Jesus' called us to make God himself the focus of our desires not heaven. He said the greatest commandment is to, "love the Lord your God with all your heart" (Mark 12:30). But how can people love someone they do not know? How can they desire someone they have not seen?

THE CAR

After getting my driver's license as a teenager, I had my heart set on a little red Honda. Four-cylinder engine, two doors, alloy wheels, a rear spoiler. It was sweet. I would daydream about it in school and collected car magazines featuring it. I *adored* that little Honda.

But adoring wasn't enough. I had to *acquire* it. I had three options—buy it myself, get someone to buy it for me, or steal it. After a year of earning minimum wage, the last option started to look appealing. Thankfully, felony was not required. My parents, who were better to me than I deserved, bought me a car that I never could have purchased on my own.

It's a silly analogy, but my quest for a life with that old Honda illustrates three essential parts of a life with God.

Why did Jesus bother with carpentry in a backwater town for thirty years? Why the years of hanging out with lepers and losers? Why all of the miracles and parables? Scripture says **Jesus didn't simply come to *die* for us; he first came to *dwell* with us** (John 1:14). There was a purpose for Jesus' life before the cross. He had something to show us. When his followers asked to see God, Jesus said, "Anyone who has seen me has seen the Father" (John 14:9, NIV). Jesus is, "the image of the invisible God...in him all the fullness of God was pleased to dwell" (Colossians 1:15, 19).

Simply put, **Jesus came to reveal who God is and what he is really like**. Everything between his birth and death was intended to show us a clear vision of God so that we might begin to **adore** him rather than fear him.

As with my Honda, adoration is not enough if we want a life with God. That is why the cross is so important. Jesus removed our evil that keeps us

from God by taking it upon himself on the cross. His death opened the way for us to be with God. **For those who desire God more than anything, the cross is the best news imaginable.** Through it we have been freely given what we never could have acquired on our own.

But for those who don't really want God, who haven't come to see his beauty, power, or goodness, the cross is useless or even ridiculous. It's like being handed the keys to a priceless Bugatti and throwing them away because you prefer taking the bus. We must recognize and adore the treasure we're being offered before we'll joyfully accept it.

After my parents gave me that little red Honda, I didn't leave it parked in the driveway. I drove it! I experienced life with my car—the rev of the exhaust and the wind in my hair (back then I still had some).

Sadly, adoring and acquiring is where some people give up their exploration of Jesus. They assume that's the end of the matter, at least on this side of eternity. They're wrong. One critical part remains. Time to fasten your seatbelt.

Q: *When have you had a clear and ravishing vision of who God is? What in your life is blocking your vision of God's goodness?*

LIVING "RADICALLY" ISN'T WHAT YOU THINK

CHAPTER

7

The Root

"How radical do I have to be?" Nicole asked me this question after reading yet another popular religious book about living "radically" for God. She confessed to feeling guilty for living an "ordinary" life in the suburbs, but also exhausted by endless calls from church leaders to reject such an existence.

Nicole was feeling the affects of a religious tradition that defines the radical life externally. It says a person's value is determined by their radicalness, and radicalness is determined by a person's circumstances. Radical *is* leaving your marketing job to vaccinate refugees in Sudan. Radical *is not* doing accounting in a cubical. Radical *is* preaching on a street corner. Radical *is not* teaching third graders math.

The call to be radical causes many to think a truly blessed life is only available to extremists. The religious view says ordinary lives, like Nicole's, are somewhere down the hierarchy of holiness. Ordinary lives are not *ungodly*, but they're clearly not "sold out" for God either.

> "The worst thing I can be is the same as everybody else. I hate that."
> ARNOLD SCHWARZENEGGER

Christians in the Greek city of Corinth held this view 2,000 years ago. They wrote to the Apostle Paul asking how they should change their ordinary circumstances in order to experience God more fully. His answer is as surprising now as it was then.

Paul completely rejected the idea that a blessed life depended upon a person's circumstances. Instead, he told everyone to stay put; to remain right where they were. **Changing your circumstances, he insisted, *does not change your relationship with God*** or your ability to experience the fullness of a life with him (see 1 Corinthians 7:17-24). According to Paul, a radical life can be lived by anyone, anywhere so long as you live there "*with* God."

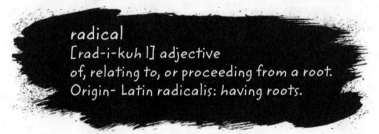

radical
[rad-i-kuh l] adjective
of, relating to, or proceeding from a root.
Origin- Latin radicalis: having roots.

The word *radical* means "root"—the *invisible* part of a plant that gives it strength and nourishment. The truly radical life, therefore, is not defined by a person's visible circumstances. Instead, radical is a life that draws strength and power from a deep, rooted, and often invisible connection with God.

That means it's possible for a minivan-driving mom in the suburbs to be living a more radical life with God than the celebrity-religious activist out to change the world.

This is the third, and most overlooked, part of Jesus' message. After **adoring** God through Jesus' life, and **acquiring** him through Jesus' death on the cross, we are also invited to **abide** with him right where we are through the power of Jesus' resurrection.

After rising from the grave and defeating the powers of evil and death, Jesus sent the Holy Spirit to dwell within his people (Acts 2). The Spirit is the presence of God to guide and comfort us. Because God now abides within us—rather than in a temple, on a mountain top, or in a refugee camp—changing our circumstances does nothing to advance or diminish our ability to experience him. That is why Paul said to remain where you are.

THE COOK

When Nicholas was 16 years old, he came to see the power and love of God through Jesus. It is said that, "he received such a high view" and "it kindled in him such a love for God" that it never faded from his soul. Some years later, Nicholas became known as Brother Lawrence, and he spent the remainder of his life working in a kitchen. Not exactly how the world defines a radical calling.

Four hundred years later, however, Brother Lawrence is still remembered for his deep, joyful connection with God. He believed, like Paul, that all of life and every circumstance was sacred. He cultivated a deep life of prayer in his kitchen. For him, cooking a meal was no different than worshipping in a cathedral. Those who thought that changing their circumstances drew them closer to God, Lawrence said, suffered from "a great delusion."

This is exactly what Paul had in mind when he said to remain where we are with God, and to "pray without ceasing" (1 Thessalonians 5:17). If that sounds impossible or exhausting, that's because you probably think of prayer

> "Men invent means and methods of coming at God's love, they learn rules and set up devices to remind them of that love, and it seems like a world of trouble.... Yet it might be so simple. Is it not quicker and easier just to do our common business wholly for the love of him?"
>
> BROTHER LAWRENCE

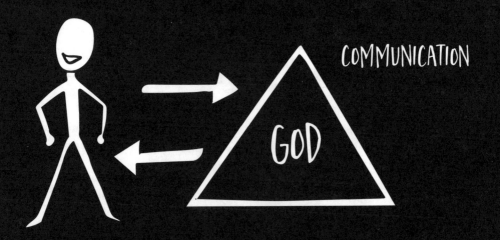

COMMUNICATION

GOD

COMMUNION

as talking to God. Some traditions believe that God also talks to us. In either case, prayer is viewed merely as communication.

Jesus saw prayer as something more. He did not experience unity with God only while speaking to him, but also in his hours of healing, teaching, and serving. He spoke of "dwelling" with his Father. "I do not speak on my own authority," Jesus said, "but the Father who dwells in me does his works. Believe me that I am in the Father and the Father is in me" (John 14:10-11).

Jesus didn't just *communicate* with his Father, he lived in constant *communion* with him. This is the kind of prayer Brother Lawrence practiced as he worked feverishly among his pots and pans. Brother Lawrence described this life of continual connection with God as so "sweet and delightful" that "those only can comprehend it who practice and experience it."

> "The issue of prayer is not prayer; the issue of prayer is God."
> ABRAHAM JOSHUA HESCHEL

One of those people was Mother Teresa, the humble nun who cared for the poor of Calcutta, India. In the 1980s she was interviewed by Dan Rather on CBS News. He asked her, "When you pray, what do you say to God?"

"I don't say anything," she replied. "I listen." Dan Rather tried the question another way.

"When God speaks to you, then, what does he say?"

"He doesn't say anything. He listens." The news anchor was baffled by her answer.

"And if you don't understand that," Mother Teresa added, "I can't explain it to you."

Imagine how different your ordinary life would be if you learned to pray without ceasing; if you put down deep roots into communion with God right where you are. It might not change your circumstances, but it will fill you with an awareness of God's presence and love that will change how you *see* your circumstances.

Q: How have you understood prayer? Is it a chore or a delight? What would help you practice prayer differently?

THE WORLD IS A PERFECTLY SAFE PLACE (REALLY)

The Eyes

Albert Einstein once said that if his life depended on solving a problem in only one hour, he would use fifty-five minutes determining the right question to ask. "Once I know the proper question," he said, "I could solve the problem in less than five minutes." Einstein understood that if we begin with the wrong question we will never arrive at the right answer.

In Chapter 1 we learned that religion begins with the question, *How do you control the world?* And each tradition or philosophy then offers a different answer. None, as we have seen, manages to deliver us from the cycle of danger, fear, and control that plagues us, and in some cases religion only makes us more afraid and the world more dangerous.

Jesus, however, started with a completely different question. He ignored *How do you control the world?*, and instead asked, *How do you see the world?*

Rather than offering his followers a new system of control through rituals or rules, Jesus wanted to give them new eyes—a new way to see the world. That doesn't mean behaviors don't matter. They matter a lot, but Jesus knew that vision determines action. **How we see the world defines how we live**

within it. If we are ever going to act with love, generosity, forgiveness, and mercy as he did, we must first see the world as he sees it.

Ask the right question.

For example, when soldiers came to arrest Jesus and his friends, Peter tried to get control over what he saw as a dangerous situation by attacking with a sword. (Being a fisherman and not a soldier he only managed to remove one guy's ear.) Jesus, however, did not resist. He did not attack. He did not run. Instead, he healed the ear of the man who came to arrest and kill him.

Jesus acted differently because he saw what Peter could not. Amid the soldiers and swords, Jesus also saw a God-with-us world. He knew that his heavenly Father was still with him, and even at a moment when darkness appeared to reign he did not have to be afraid because ultimately everything would be okay.

Whether sailing through a storm, facing soldiers in a garden, or not having any lunch money, Peter and the other disciples were constantly afraid. Jesus' miracles and parables were designed to open their eyes. He wanted them to see a world in which fear was unnecessary because they were perfectly safe with God.

"When God loves you, what can be better than that?"
ARETHA FRANKLIN

The Sermon

"Do you think Jesus was serious?" I asked a classroom of thirty adults that question after reading the Sermon on the Mount together. The sermon (found in Matthew 5-7) contains many of Jesus' best known teachings including the commands to forgive, turn the other cheek, and love your enemy. With a show of hands the class voted 30-0. They *did not* think Jesus was serious. "Why not?" I asked.

"It's not possible to live that way."

"Jesus was just exaggerating to make a point."

"The world will walk all over you if you do that stuff."

I was amazed at the lengths these committed churchgoers went to dismiss Jesus' commands especially given that he concluded the Sermon on the Mount with a warning about the danger of not obeying his words (Matthew 7:24-27). Most of the class admired the beauty and idealism of the sermon, but it appeared detached from reality because they still saw the world as a very dangerous place. Therefore, the call to give freely, bless your enemy, and live without anger could only be dismissed as hyperbole or rejected as madness.

Most Christians, like everyone else, expect religion to provide ways to control a dangerous world. That's why the Sermon on the Mount makes no sense to them. It offers no control. Instead, Jesus' message accepts one simple fact: **control is an illusion.** You don't have it and you never will, and no amount of control will make you safe or eliminate your fears. So, any religious system promising you control is either delusional or dangerously deceptive. As Jesus said in his sermon, "which of you by being anxious [worrying] can add a single hour to his life?" (Matthew 6:27).

> "If everything seems under control you're just not going fast enough."
> MARIO ANDRETTI

If control is not possible, how do we overcome our fears and break the cycle? This is where living with God makes all the difference. **As we come to**

A **SAFE WORLD**

A **DANGEROUS WORLD**

SURRENDER CONTROL	DEMAND CONTROL
LOVE YOUR ENEMY	HATE YOUR ENEMY
GIVE GENEROUSLY	GIVE SPARINGLY
SEEK TO FORGIVE	SEEK TO AVENGE
TAKE UP YOUR CROSS	TAKE UP YOUR RIGHTS

JESUS IS...

MASTER   A **MORON**

see God clearly and experience his unending goodness we discover a life-changing truth— we are perfectly safe in his hands.

When the Apostle John came to the end of his long life, he summarized Jesus' entire message this way: "God is light, and in him is no darkness at all" (1 John 1:5). Jesus brought the good news that God can be trusted. Always. And he proved it by trusting his Father even to the point of death knowing he would raise him back to life. Jesus showed that not even death can separate us from God's love (Romans 8:38-39). If that is true, then we are absolutely safe in this world.

It's a theme that runs throughout Jesus' sermon. From the beginning where he explains how God blesses those the world rejects, to the middle where he explains how much our heavenly Father loves us, to the end where he says those living with God don't have to be afraid of the world's storms— the entire sermon and all of its commands are addressed to people who have been set free from fear because they see and know God's goodness.

"In this is love, not that we loved God but that he loved us and sent his Son to be the propitiation [payment] for our sins."
1 JOHN 4:10

Only when we have a clear and ravishing vision of God's goodness will we see the world as a safe place, and only when we are assured of our safety will we find the power to serve, forgive, bless, and love even our enemies. This power over fear that comes to us when we see with new eyes has another name—*faith*.

The Trapeze

Henri Nouwen, a Dutch priest, professor, and author, saw the truth about faith through the Flying Rodleighs, a trapeze troupe. Nouwen noticed that while everyone is focused on the flyer's arial acrobatics, he's really not the star of the performance. They forget that the flyer's amazing act is only possible because he knows he will be safely caught. Everything depends

> "If we are to take risks, to be free, in the air, in life, we have to know there's a catcher. We have to know that when we come down from it all, we're going to be caught, we're going to be safe. The great hero is the least visible. Trust the catcher."
>
> HENRI NOUWEN

upon the other trapeze artist, the catcher. This led Nouwen to a new way of understanding living with God.

Faith is the opposite of seeking control; faith is willfully surrendering it. Faith is letting go and trusting that we will be caught. It is, "the assurance of thing hoped for, the conviction of things not seen" (Hebrews 11:1) It's the promise that no matter what happens God will not let us fall. With this assurance we are free to let go, we are free to soar. We are free to love others without being restrained by fear or preoccupied with our own safety, and we can do this with the peace and joy that come from the hope that God will catch us.

Once we are caught, however, and we're safely in God's hands, faith and hope are no longer necessary. All that remains is love.

Q: What do you sense God calling you to do? What fear is keeping you from trusting him?

ALL YOU NEED IS LOVE

CHAPTER
9

THE HOUND

Jesus spoke frequently about love, but not the spineless, sentimental sort one finds in greeting cards or on un-reality television. He spoke of a gritty, ferocious, unrelenting love that never stops seeking what is good for others even when they resist its pursuit. Francis Thompson, a nineteenth century poet who battled poverty, depression, and drug addiction, spoke of God's relentless love as the "Hound of Heaven" that hunts us down until we are finally snatched in its jaws.

Martin Luther King, Jr. experienced this tenacious love of God. On a winter night in 1956, while leading a bus boycott in Montgomery, Alabama, King received a threatening phone call. The voice vowed to kill King and his family if he did not leave town. Unable to sleep, he poured himself a cup of coffee and sat down at the kitchen table. King later admitted to being "scared to death" and "paralyzed by fear."

Dr. King didn't know it as he sat alone in his dark kitchen, but he was being pursued by more than the Klu Klux Klan. The Hound of Heaven was also at his heels. With his face buried in his hands over his coffee, King said he heard an inner voice. The Spirit of God said to him, "Stand up for righteousness. Stand up for justice. Stand up for truth, and lo, I will be with you, even until the end of the world." Reflecting on the encounter years later in a sermon, King said God promised, "never to leave me, never to leave me alone. No, never alone. He promised to never leave me, never to leave me alone."

At that moment in his kitchen, King said his fear disappeared and a supernatural courage took its place. God's love led him to declare, "I can stand up without fear. I can face anything."

The Hound wasn't finished. Three nights later King's house was bombed. Thankfully everyone escaped unharmed, but an angry mob of African-Americans gathered with weapons ready to retaliate. King stood on the porch of his smoldering house and addressed the crowd by quoting Jesus:

> "He who lives by the sword shall die by the sword. I want you to love your enemies. Be good to them. Love them and let them know you love them. For we doing what is right. We are doing what is just. And God is with us."
> MARTIN LUTHER KING, JANUARY 30, 1956

The fear and anger that had filled the crowd disappeared. They dropped their guns, held hands, and began to sing. The Hound of Heaven had struck again.

The Siege

Thomas Aquinas, a thirteenth-century theologian, saw fear as a contracting force upon the soul. **Fear shrinks our heart and draws us into a posture of self-obsession.** This is what Martin Luther King, Jr. experienced at his kitchen table when he was "paralyzed by fear." By his own admission, King was fixated on protecting himself and his family rather than advancing the justice of God or loving his enemies.

Aquinas compared a fearful person to a medieval city under siege. As the enemy's

> "Fear is such a powerful emotion for humans that when we allow it to take us over, it drives compassion right out of our hearts."
> THOMAS AQUINAS

LOVE

FEAR

ENEMY

"THERE IS NO FEAR IN LOVE, BUT PERFECT LOVE CASTS OUT FEAR." –1 JOHN 4:18

army advanced, the inhabitants of the countryside would quickly gather food and supplies and retreat behind the city's walls. With its gates closed and defenses up, the city would hope its stockpiled resources outlasted those of the enemy surrounding it. (The longest siege in history lasted for 22 years!)

Likewise, when filled with fear we draw all of our energy and resources inward. Fixated on our own survival, we become incapable of empathy or generosity. We live behind walls and keep others at a distance.

This siege imagery explains why religions often talk about love but struggle to display it. **Being rooted in fear and control, religion causes us to turn inward and become defensive toward outsiders or threatened by those who are different.** This can be seen among individuals and entire communities as religious people continue to build wall in a foolish quest for safety.

> "Fear engenders fear.
> It never gives birth to love."
> HENRI NOUWEN

The love of Jesus, however, ends the siege and breaks down the walls. It was this love that broke King's paralysis and gave him the courage to love his enemies. Or consider Francis of Assisi who lived during the Crusades of the thirteenth century when Christian empires in the West clashed with Muslim empires in the East. In 1219, during a battle against for forces of Sultan Malik al-Kamil in Egypt, Francis defied the commander of the Crusader army and crossed the battlefield to speak with the Sultan directly. Francis was warned that the Sultan was a merciless monster, and that he would be tortured and killed if he entered the enemy's camp.

Filled with love rather than fear, Francis went anyway. He crossed the battle lines wearing only a robe, barefoot and unarmed. Amazed, and probably confused, the Muslim soldiers brought him before the Sultan. "May the Lord give you peace," Francis said, and introduced himself as "an ambassador of Jesus" rather than as a representative of the Crusader army, a European king, or the Pope.

Recognizing Francis as a man of peace and not war, the Sultan invited him to stay as his guest. For days they shared meals and exchanged ideas. The Sultan, it turned out, was not an uncivilized tyrant, but a philosophical man with an open mind. He desired to know more about Jesus from the fearless Francis, and Francis humbly learned from the Sultan.

With a spirit of hospitality and mutual respect, the two men created an oasis of peace during a century of conflict. **Where religion erects walls and ignites wars, the love of Jesus removes barriers and brings healing**. Isn't that what our world needs today?

Prayer of Francis of Assisi

Lord, make me an instrument of your peace.
Where there is hatred, let me sow love;
Where there is injury, pardon;
Where there is doubt, faith;
Where there is despair, hope;
Where there is darkness, light;
Where there is sadness, joy.

O Divine Master, grant that I may not so much seek
To be consoled as to console,
To be understood as to understand,
To be loved as to love;
For it is in giving that we receive;
It is in pardoning that we are pardoned;
It is in dying to self that we are born to eternal life.

The Beloved

Have you ever seen an apple tree produce pears or a grapevine produce cherries? Of course not. A plant can only produce what it is. Jesus said people are the same way. **You cannot produce what you do not possess.** Francis of Assisi, Martin Luther King, Jr., Mother Theresa, and Brother Lawrence were able to display the relentless, courageous love of God because they were filled with that love as they lived *with* God. The power to love others is available to us, the Apostle John said, only because God first loved us (1 John 4:19).

That's the key to everything. Before we can break through our barricades of fear, before we can escape endless cycles of danger and control, before we can overcome what's wrong with religion to create a better world, we must first know the love of God ourselves. That doesn't happen by listening to a sermon or reading a book (even one with stick figures and flow

> "All of humanity's problems stem from man's inability to sit quietly in a room alone."
> PASCAL

116

charts). **Knowing God's love means *experiencing* it, and that means learning to be still.**

In silence and solitude the hidden things of our souls begin to surface, including our fears and attempts at control. We face the discomfort of our own evil and selfish desires as they emerge from the shadows. The anger, shame, guilt, and grief that we've pushed to the background with endless activities and flickering screens comes rushing at us. In silence we are knocked down by the overwhelming noise of our inner lives.

If we stay there long enough, however, something remarkable happens. The inner voices telling us we are not safe enough, smart enough, good enough, beautiful enough, successful enough, popular enough; all of the voices of religion and culture tempting us to seek more control begin to fade away as the only voice that really matters speaks the only truth we need to hear. God meets us in the silence and whispers, "You are loved."

You are ████████ are ██████████████████

████████████████████████████████████

██████████████████████████████████████

██████████████████████████████████████

██████████████████████████████████████

██████████████████████████████████████

██████████████████████████████████████

██████████████████████████████████████

██████████████████████████████████████

██████████████████████████████████████

██████████████████████ loved ██████████

██████████████████████████████████████

██████████████████████████████████████

Henri Nouwen described the importance of being with God alone this way:

> *To pray is to listen to the One who calls you "my beloved daughter," "my beloved son," "my beloved child." To pray is to let that voice speak to the center of your being, to your guts, and let that voice resound in your whole being. If you keep that in mind, you can deal with an enormous amount of success as well as an enormous amount of failure without losing your identity, because your identity is that you are the beloved. Long before your father and mother, your brothers and sisters, your teachers, your church, or any people touched you in a loving as well as in a wounding way—long before you were rejected by some person or praised by somebody else—that voice has been there always. "I have loved you with an everlasting love." That love was there before you were born and will be there after you die.*
>
> Henri Nouwen, "From Solitude to Community to Ministry," *Leadership Journal*, Spring 1995.

Now that we have reached the end of the book, I hope you can recognize what is wrong with religion and what is so wonderful about Jesus. My great hope is that you will come to know the freedom and peace of living *with* God rather than merely living *for* him, and that in seeing his infinite worth you will hear his voice declaring yours.

Next Steps

> Get alone with God and listen for his voice.

> Read the Gospel of John

> Sign up for With God Daily at SkyeJethani.com

> Talk to someone who knows Jesus

> Identify your fears

> Share this book with a friend

Books About Living With God

- Skye Jethani: *With*

- Brother Lawrence:
  The Practice of the Presence of God

- Richard J. Foster: *Prayer*

- N.T. Wright: *Simply Jesus*

- Henri Nouwen:
  The Return of the Prodigal Son

- A.W. Tozer: *The Pursuit of God*

QUESTIONS?

I'd love to help you figure out faith.
Email your questions to me at:

ReligionBook@SkyeJethani.com

Get Skye Jethani on your smartphone.

With God » DAILY

Start every day with a reflection written by Skye, readings from scripture, and historic prayers to guide your own communion with God.

Sign up at www.WithGodDaily.com

ALSO BY SKYE JETHANI

WITH
Reimagining the Way You Relate to God

FUTUREVILLE
Discover Your Purpose for Today by Reimagining Tomorrow

THE DIVINE COMMODITY
Discovering a Faith Beyond Consumer Christianity

Get these and more resources at SkyeJethani.com

Notes

NOTES

Notes